# LITTLE BOOK OF THE
# SIX NATIONS

Written by Graeme Kent

# LITTLE BOOK OF THE
# SIX NATIONS

This edition first published in the UK in 2008
By Green Umbrella Publishing

© Green Umbrella Publishing 2008

Publishers Jules Gammond and Vanessa Gardner

Printed and bound in Italy

ISBN 978-1-905828-50-0

# Contents

| | | |
|---|---|---|
| 4 – 07 | The Carrying Game | (1871-1909) |
| 18 – 35 | In and Out | (1910-1931) |
| 36 – 49 | Back to Basics | (1932-1946) |
| 50 – 63 | Post War | (1947-1968) |
| 64 – 77 | Years of the Dragon | (1969-1980) |
| 78 – 105 | England Emerges – Briefly | (1981-1999) |
| 106 – 121 | The Six Nations | (2000-2007) |
| 122 – 125 | Appendix | |

# Chapter 1

# The Carrying Game (1871-1909)

THE FIRST INTERNATIONAL HOME Countries rugby football match was played at Edinburgh between Scotland and England on 27th March 1871. There were twenty players on each side and two umpires patrolling the touch-lines, instead of a referee on the field. The England side travelled to Scotland by train in the third class compartment, paying their own expenses. Scotland won by two tries to a goal.

One of the features of the game were the struggles between the two thirteen-man packs, some of which lasted for up to five minutes before the ball emerged. Three half-backs were expected to lurk behind the melee and attempt to scamper off hopefully upfield with the ball on the rare occasions that it appeared.

The English side darkly suspected the Scots of an early example of games-manship when they discovered that the pitch was only 55 yards wide, much smaller than the dimensions to which it was accustomed.

This first match between the two nations had been the result of an adver-tisement placed by a group of Scottish players in The Scotsman and Bell's Life in London, challenging England to play them at 'the carrying game'. Subsequent international matches were organised by the newly formed English Rugby Football Union. The next year England reversed the first result and a series of international matches between the two nations was under way.

A trophy to be competed for annually

was presented by the about-to-become defunct Calcutta Rugby Club, when its expatriate members had all the silver rupees left in its account melted down and made into the Calcutta Cup. One of the members of the club instrumental in the decision was a Scot, B.H. Burns, a member of the Blackheath side, who had played for England in the very first rugby international against Scotland in 1870. The ornate trophy was carved by Indian craftsmen, with depictions of cobras for handles and a lid surmounted by an elephant.

From the very beginning guile was used off the pitch as well as on it. In 1873 England travelled to the west of Scotland for a match only to discover that the pitch was very muddy. At once the away side sent its boots to a local cobbler, with orders for leather bars to be affixed to the soles to negate the slippery conditions. When the boots were returned just before the game it was discovered that two of them were missing. A member of the Scottish side later wrote gleefully, 'the boots and feet could not be got to correspond.' Whether the shoemaker was inefficient or excessively patriotic was never established. Whatever the reason, two of the English players were forced to play in one football boot and one of the ordinary variety. As the years passed, the laws and tactics of the game changed and national bodies were set up to administrate and oversee games between the four Home Countries of England, Scotland, Ireland and Wales. In 1875, Ireland challenged England and two years later played against Scotland. Ireland's second match against England was marked by a try from Dublin University student A.P. Cronyn, who picked up the ball close to his own touchline and ran the length of the field to score, despite the fact that his jersey had been torn off in practically the first tackle he had received.

For some time the Irish selection process was handicapped by the political divide and the fact that the Dublin rugby organising body insisted on picking ten of the players and the Belfast union the other ten.

In 1883, Wales travelled to England. During the 1882-83 season, all the home countries played against one another, except that Wales did not play Ireland. Even so, this season is generally regarded as the first International Championship. The following season all four nations played against one another. Several years later the English R.F.U. decided that the value of a try should

be one point and a conversion another two points. The other nations were slow to accept this change and games were sometimes played with two versions of scoring. In 1891 it was agreed that the value of a try should be two points. Several years later this was upgraded to three points.

For a decade after this England and Scotland were the strongest rugby-playing countries. The England side was dominated by middle-class players. There were nine Oxford undergraduates in one team of the period. Ireland was the most successful team once, in 1888, although it was a muted achievement as England did not play this season and Ireland won only one of the two games it played. Wales generally remained at the foot of the table. There were many more clubs in England than in any of the other Home Countries, and for some time this was reflected in the calibre of the players it turned out.

The game was still in its early stages and for years there were many changes and anomalies. These were highlighted at the international level in the 1880s and 1890s, when different international cultures, as well as teams, clashed. Once the size of teams had been reduced

England v. Scotland
~ March 13th 1886 ~

J E Stoddart    H Bonsor    A Teggin    E B Brutton
C Gurdon    A Rotherham    W G Clibborn    N Spurling    R Robertshaw
F E Ingles    E T Gurdon    E Wilkinson    C J B Marriott
C H Sample    G L Jeffery

**ABOVE** England rugby team of 1886

to fifteen, international sides usually played two full-backs, two wing three-quarters, two half backs and nine forwards. This system was thrown out of balance in 1893, when Wales, playing with four three-quarters, defeated Scotland, causing the other nations to rethink and overhaul their playing systems.

One of the first attacking wing three-quarters under the new system was the greatest all-round athlete of his age, A.E. Stoddart, who represented England at rugby and cricket. Later in life he was to kill himself in a fit of depression.

As the game began to sort itself out, referees were still something of an afterthought in those first days of rugby football. The relevant article in the first code issued by the R.F.U. stated intriguingly, 'The captains of the respective sides shall be the sole arbiters of all disputes.' This meant that if the captains could not agree one of them would lead his side off the field in a high dudgeon.

At first each side provided its own umpire to control an international. The two officials were supposed to work in harmony, but this did not always prove to be the case. After the drawn game between England and Scotland at Raeburn Place in 1881, the President of the Scottish Rugby Union declared sourly that England's main strength had been in its umpiring.

For some years there was as much petulance and antagonism between the governing bodies as there was on the pitch. In 1885, Scotland refused to play England because of a dispute over a try in the previous season's match. The ball had been 'fisted' back in a lineout, and when the Scottish players stopped to protest the English had scored. Ireland and Wales also fell out and would not play against each other. This meant that each side could only play two games, against the nations its controlling body happened to be talking to at the time. In 1886, the four countries somewhat reluctantly resumed the full tournament, although it was to prove a temporary arrangement.

In the following year Ireland celebrated the resumption of the competition by achieving its first victory in thirteen outings against England. The Irish magazine Sport devoted part of its next issue to a parody of the music hall song Two Lovely Black Eyes in honour of the occasion: Two goals off two tries Oh, what a surprise; Were ever Englishmen leathered like this? Two goals off two tries.

To prevent unseemly squabbles the home unions of Ireland, Scotland and Wales hastily formed the International Rugby Football Board, more than a century later to become the I.R.B. This body was intended to adjudicate in any

# THE CARRYING GAME

disputes between the Home Countries. England at once refused to join, giving as its reason the fact that as it had more clubs than the other nations it should have more seats on the newly formed committee. This time it walked out of the competition altogether and did not return for two years. Until 1890, the only international match England played was against a touring New Zealand Maori side.

It was finally mollified by the offer of six seats on the board of the I.R.F.U. compared with the two allotted to each of the other Home Countries. The offer was accepted grudgingly and England condescended to resume its place in the tournament in 1890. To rub it in, England immediately won the title again, losing only to Wales that season.

Despite these altercations the standard of rugby was improving all the time and there were some spectacular internationals played. In 1893, Wales defeated England by a single point at Cardiff Arms Park on a pitch that had to be defrosted overnight by fifty coal fires in braziers. Wales lined up with four three-quarters and eight forwards against England's nine forwards and three three-quarters. Wales

went on to win the Triple Crown for the first time that season.

Just as the format of international rugby was being worked out on the pitch, many of the pioneer players were performing with an equal degree of individualism. The Irish full-back D.B. Walkington was reputed to play with a monocle in his eye, although it was conceded that he sometimes removed it before making a tackle. It was not long, either before the physiques and off-field activities of some of the players were being reflected in their nicknames, as was the case of the Irish three-quarter Larry Bulger, who was known far and wide as the Fat Cupid.

On a more serious note one of the pioneers of change on the pitch was an Oxford undergraduate, Alan Rotherham, who played a dozen times for England in the 1880s and revolutionised half-back play. A contemporary marvelled of his pioneering thinking, 'He was the first to clearly demonstrate that a half-back ought not to run and play for himself, but ought essentially to be the connecting link between the forwards and three-quarters.'

Always the selectors had to be able to think on their feet and have wide-ranging contacts. On a number of occasions travelling international sides turned up for games short of a few players who had cried off at the last moment or who had lost their way on the journey to the match. It became customary to fill the gaps with any available nationals working away from home, or even with reserves from the host nation.

Youth was certainly no bar to selection. A number of schoolboys played international rugby during this period. In 1903, Ken Mcleod, a 15-year-old pupil at Fettes College was selected to play on the wing for Scotland against Wales. This would have made him the youngest ever international. His headmaster refused to allow him time off from his studies. Mcleod had to wait two more years for the first of his ten caps.

The Scots always had a desperately small base from which to select their players. The Reverend P. Anton, who played for his country in the 1890s wrote, 'With the exception of the St Andrews University, there was not a single club north of the Forth, and south of the Tweed, only four other clubs of notable pretensions.'

In an early example of the cult of personality, some international players, however, began to accumulate important admirers. In 1895, the half-back Aloysius Mary (Louis) Magee made the first of 27 international appearances for Ireland, against England. He was to become so idolised in his home country that the great novelist James Joyce mentioned him approvingly in his groundbreaking book Ulysses.

The fame of the game was certainly spreading to unlikely quarters. Before the end of the century even the aesthetic playwright Oscar Wilde was moved to take notice of the sport, commenting disparagingly, 'Rugby is a good occasion for keeping thirty bullies away from the centre of the city.'

The more boisterous of the post-match celebrations also began to be noticed by the press. As early as 1873, an England player was apprehended after an international happily driving a purloined mail cart through Glasgow's streets in the small hours of the morning. The day after the Dublin match between Ireland and Wales in 1890 saw nine players fined for riotous behaviour.

Referees, when umpires were discarded, did not have an easy life. They were not even equipped with whistles

until 1885. In the same decade two Irish players stalked off the pitch at Lansdowne Road because of decisions made by the Welsh umpire. At Blackheath the Irish referee was harangued for ten minutes by Scottish players objecting to a try he had awarded to England. In 1892, the official had to be hustled off the field at Swansea by a posse of protective Welsh players after the home crowd objected to some of the decisions he had given in Wales' defeat to Scotland. One of the home side players was struck by enraged

members of the mob for coming to the aid of the arbiter.

In sheer self-defence the officials could hardly be blamed for becoming both autocratic and idiosyncratic upon occasion. Their behaviour ranged from one who refereed a match in white boots and a very well cut overcoat to any number prudently delaying the final whistle until they were opposite the players' tunnel down which they could then flee to the comparative safety of the dressing room.

Despite, or perhaps because of these events, international rugby union football became increasingly popular. Four thousand spectators had watched the first-ever international. By 1899, a crowd of 40,000 watched the Wales v. Ireland match at Cardiff Arms Park, in the season when the visitors defeated the other three nations in the tournament. This seems to have been the first occasion upon which the term Triple Crown was used in newspapers for such a feat.

Pitches were not prepared with quite the same degree of care as later became the case, but the players were both pragmatic and adaptable. When the Llanelli field was said to be too hard for a Wales-England international, the match was transferred equably to an adjacent cricket ground, although some spectators grumbled at having to make the trek across in such inhospitable conditions.

Uneasily the Four Nations tournament played its full complement of games each season until 1897, but towards the end of this period its stability was threatened yet again. From the eccentrics and wild men on the field, the first rugby superstars had begun to emerge, sometimes bringing trouble with them. The catalyst in this latest upheaval was a man known to rugby fans as 'Monkey'.

The best known of the early internationals was the Welshman Arthur Gould. Dubbed 'Monkey' for his childhood hobby of climbing trees, Gould was good-looking, fast, elusive and could kick with either foot. His career lasted from 1882 until 1898. He established a record of scoring 37 tries in 24 games for his club in the 1892-83 season. He played 27 times for Wales, usually as a centre, and was so popular that a public subscription, backed by the Welsh Rugby Union, raised £700 to buy him a cottage.

**LEFT** Welsh Rugby team of 1895

# THE CARRYING GAME

Unfortunately this gesture was almost to destroy the always precarious state of international rugby relations. Already worried by the insidious threat of professionalism in the sport, the other national unions claimed that Gould's testimonial had rendered him a professional player. Gould attempted to defuse the situation by announcing his retirement. The Scottish Rugby Union in particular refused to accept the centre's offer. Suddenly, for different reasons, the Home Countries seemed to be at loggerheads with one another on and off the field once more.

Declaring that by condoning the Gould affair the Welsh Rugby Union was supporting professionalism, Scotland refused to play the principality in the following season. This meant that in 1898 only England and Ireland played their full three games each. England headed the championship with a win, a loss and a draw, while Ireland, who had won the championship two years earlier, took the Wooden Spoon.

The Gould matter brought to a head the long-simmering matter of professionalism in rugby. For some time, especially in the north of England, it had been the policy to offer 'broken time' to better players, making up the wages they had lost while playing for their clubs. Increasingly pressure was being brought on the club committees to ban such a practice. This caused enormous resentment between the associations whose players were largely middle class and could afford to take time off, and those, mainly in the north, with members who could not afford to lose wages when they played.

In 1895, 22 of the northern clubs met at the George Hotel in Huddersfield to discuss the matter of payment. They voted to leave the Rugby Football Union and set up their own controlling body, the Northern Rugby Football Union, allowing payments to players. This association later became the professional Rugby Football League and caused a great regional and philosophical split in the game.

The northern defection was a severe blow, especially to England, which was no longer getting everything its own way on the field as the other nations improved. England had depended greatly on its northern players. In one match alone eight Yorkshire men had been in the side. From 1895, the year of the secession, until 1910 England did not win the championship once. Other nations were quick to fill the breach. From 1900, Wales won six titles before England struggled back into contention.

There was one unexpected occurrence in Welsh rugby during this period. In 1904, during a brief resurgence of Methodist religious fervour in parts of the country, rugby was attacked as inciting sinful passions of aggression. To emphasise the point there was a staged public tearing up of international tickets. On a wider front a major change in the competition was on the horizon. The Four Nations were about to become the Five Nations.

# What Did They Say?

*'When the umpire is in doubt, I think he is justified in deciding against the side which makes the most noise!'*

**H.H. Almond, one of the umpires in the first international, between England and Scotland in 1871.**

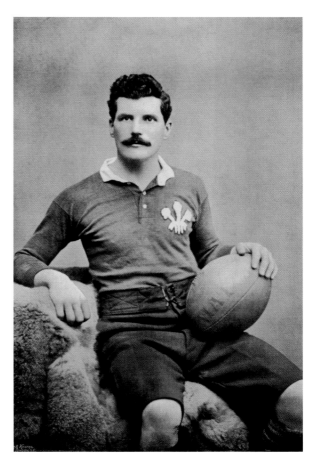

# Chapter 2

# In and Out (1910-1931)

RUGBY FOOTBALL WAS FIRST TAKEN to France in the early 1870s by a group of expatriate wine merchants working in Le Havre, although the game they indulged in seems to have been a mixture of rugby and football. Five years later, the genuine game was being played by several clubs in Paris. By 1900, the game had developed to such an extent that France won the rugby gold medal at the Paris Olympics held that year. In 1906, a touring New Zealand side was played and soon France was invited to join what then became the Five Nations tournament.

Its baptism was a fiery one. In their first game, against Wales, they lost by 49-14, and in that first season they went on to lose all four matches, conceding 95 points.

In that same period England played its first game at Twickenham, against Wales. One player in the England side, Harry Berry, had learned his rugby while guarding Boer prisoners of war on the remote Atlantic stronghold of St Helena in 1900. He was one of four players in the England side that day to die in the First World War.

The Twickenham ground, a market garden, had been purchased for a little over £5000 several years before by an R.F.U. committee member, and because of its original use was known as 'Billy Williams' Cabbage Patch.' In the opening matches spectators had to stand on bales of straw in order to get a better view. Eighteen thousand spectators attended the first international there, earning the R.F.U. a much-appreciated profit of £2000.

The gifted Cornish player, Bert Solomon, showed up well in the match, his first for his country. He scored a try, but declined to play for his country again because it was too far to travel to London just to play rugby. The start to the match was dramatic. In the first minute of the game, Adrian Stoop, the scrum-half, caught the Welsh kick-off and hoofed the ball back far up the field. The speedy English winger, F.E. Chapman, playing his first game for his country, chased the ball, scooped it up and scored.

Stoop, a long-serving Harlequins captain, was put in charge of England and immediately demanded that his players concentrated on passing and keeping the ball in play for comparatively long periods, another innovation and one not always appreciated by the less well-trained among his national forwards. He also insisted that the fly-half and scrum-half positions should not be interchangeable, as had hitherto been the case.

In the second season of the Five Nations, Wales won the first official Grand Slam, defeating each of the other countries. Its pack, known as 'the Terrible Eight', was led by a fiery clergyman, the Reverend Alban Davies, who had played for Oxford University. Between 1900 and 1913,

the country remained undefeated at home, but England was slowly coming back into the reckoning.

The laws of the game were becoming much more settled and cohesive, but there was still plenty of time for differing interpretations, and the referees of the period proved to be anything but automatons.

With so many different laws and interpretations it was small wonder that some of the early Five Nations internationals were controlled with a loose rein, not to say outright eccentricity. During these early years, one referee solved the problems of a recalcitrant scrum by booting its erring members up their backsides every time they packed down. Another became so exasperated with a French side's inability to put the ball into the scrum correctly, that he took over the scrum-half's duties and performed the operation himself.

The tournament continued to be a struggle for France. It scored just a solitary win, by a single point against Scotland in Paris in 1911. The game was marked by the fact that some fans smuggled cockerels into the stadium and released them joyfully at the final whistle, a tradition that was to persevere for decades. This result was all the more commendable considering the panic that ensued behind the scenes before the game. A Frenchman selected to play on the wing had left his train at a stop to buy a sandwich, only to witness with horror the engine steaming out of the station as he emerged munching from the buffet.

At the stadium the French authorities then looked for the official reserve, only to discover that he, too, had missed the train on the way to Paris. The appalled French had been reduced to begging someone in the crowd to turn out for them, when, at the last minute the reserve turned up panting at the dressing-room door.

French home crowds were not slow to express their disapproval of their team's lack of success, drawing several rebukes from the R.F.U. for inconsistency of control at home matches and for at least one attack on a referee which led to a mob rampaging through the capital, causing considerable damage to property. The R.F.U. threatened to stop supplying referees for matches involving France but later relented. Despite these problems the game remained very pop-

**LEFT** Aerial view of Twickenham, 1925

**RIGHT** The Welsh rugby team February, 1911

English Team. v Scotland at Twickenham. 1928

H.G.Periton. C.D.Aarvold. K.J.Stark. J.Hanley. F.D.Prentice. G.V.Palmer. T.H.Vile (Referee)

W.H.Taylor. J.V.Richardson. E.Stanbury. R.Cove-Smith. J.S.Tucker. T.W.Brown. R.H.Sparks.
(Captain)

H.C.C.Laird. A.T.Young.

ular in the country, with attendances of 25,000 for the home games against Scotland in 1913 and Wales in 1914.

Due to its public school antecedents, much of the game remained resolutely middle-class and amateur, especially after the break with the northern clubs. This was shown after one early Scotland-Ireland match.

A Scottish player embarked almost immediately for the Sudan, to take up a waiting appointment as a district commissioner. There he presented his international cap to a local chieftain, who wore it proudly on ceremonial occasions for many years. Some less affluent players still found it difficult to reconcile rugby with full-time employment. It was an era in which employers were extremely reluctant to allow members of their workforce time off to play mere games, even at the highest level. Employees had to guard their precious free time jealously, using every moment of it to the maximum advantage.

There were at least two examples of players combining travelling to away internationals with their honeymoons, but the ultimate sacrifice was surely made by John Macaulay of Ireland, a miller's agent. He had already used up all his annual leave when he received a summons to play for his country against England. His firm, however, did allow special time off with pay for employees getting married. It is said that the fiscally cautious Macaulay made the ultimate sacrifice in order to preserve his salary and gain a cap. He proposed marriage, later taking his very understanding bride along to the match with him on his now officially sanctioned period of leave.

There was also considerable trouble in the Ireland-Wales match of 1914, which was described as one of the dirtiest internationals ever played. Trouble started in a Belfast hotel the previous evening, when the two packs almost clashed. In one of the first recorded examples of international rugby 'sledging', the Ireland pack leader, Dr. William Tyrell, told the Welsh forward Percy Jones, 'It's you and me for it tomorrow!' to which the Welshman replied placidly, 'I shall be with you, doing the best I can.' Tyrell went on to become an air vice-marshal in the fledgling Royal Air Force.

The animosity was taken onto the field the next day. When the Reverend Alban Davies was asked why he did not put a stop to the foul language being used all

**LEFT** The England team before the match against Scotland, 1928

around him, the Welsh captain protested piously that he had heard nothing untoward through his scrum- cap.

Meanwhile, a resurgent England won back to-back Grand Slams in 1913 and 1914. During this period W.J.A. Davies played the first of 22 games for England and was never on the losing side in a championship match. Like all other players he had an enforced stoppage after the first few games because upon the outbreak of the First World War the Five Nations tournament was abandoned until 1920.

Two players in the games played during this period typified the tragedy that was about to engulf the world. Centres on opposite sides in the 1913 match between England and France were Marcel Burgun and Ronnie Poulton-Palmer. The latter had scored five tries for Oxford against Cambridge. Three years later both were dead, killed in action in France and Belgium respectively. The Times called Poulton-Palmer 'probably the greatest player of all time.' Uniquely for a rugby player, Poulton-Palmer's death at the hands of a sniper merited a poem by Alfred Ollivant in the Spectator in 1915:

*Ronald is dead; and we shall watch no more His swerving swallow-flight adown the field Amid eluded enemies...*

Rugby players from all five nations served with courage and distinction between 1914 and 1918 in the First World War. Many internationals lost their lives in the conflict. Scotland lost 30 pre-war rugby representatives, 27 England players were killed, France suffered 23 deaths among its internationals, Wales had 11 killed and nine Irish players were lost in action. One England international, E.R. Mobbs, was said to have led charges across No Man's Land by kicking a rugby ball ahead of him. Upon the outbreak of the war, within 48 hours he had recruited a 'sportsman's battalion' of over 250 men to join the Northamptonshire Regiment.

When the Five Nations resumed in 1920, Wales, England and Scotland shared the first post-war title, with three wins and a loss each. France, who finished fourth in the table, had the consolation of securing its first Five Nations victory in 17 outings, defeating Wales 6-5.

The unluckiest player of this international season was W.S. Lowry, who turned up for his first game for

**LEFT** Welsh and French teams line up at the 1920 Five Nations tournament

England, was awarded his cap, participated in the team photograph and was then dropped in favour of another winger who was considered better suited to the muddy conditions. The last-minute decision was vindicated when the replacement, H.L.V. Day, scored a try and converted it. Lowry was selected, and this time played, in a match later in the season.

The 1923 Wales-Scotland match in Cardiff contained one unfortunate incident when the Scottish centre Archie Gracie scored a try with such velocity that the force of his rush carried him over the dead ball line into a boy in the crowd, who lost several teeth in the collision.

A glittering career was launched at this time when Irishman George Stephenson was first selected to play for his country. At the beginning of the season he had been in his university's third team. He went on to play for Ireland for nine seasons without missing a match. In 1924, Ireland selected its youngest ever player, 17-year-old Frank Hewitt, who rewarded the selectors by scoring a try in a 13-10 victory over Wales.

National styles were beginning to emerge and the Scottish team was much lauded for the ferocious attacks of their

forwards dribbling the ball ahead of them in a mass, to concerted shouts of 'Feet! Feet!' from their supporters.

The England-Wales match of 1922 saw the innovation of numbered jerseys being used by both nations. It was also a time of selectors' jitters for England, with 26 players being used over the four games. In the same season the flying winger, Eric Liddell, first played for Scotland, against France. He retired from international rugby the following year to concentrate on athletics. The year after that, in the same stadium where he had made his Scottish rugby debut, Stade Colombes, he was to win a gold medal in the Olympic Games 400 metres, before dying as a missionary in China at the age of 43.

Five Nations forward play received a considerable impetus with the arrival of Wavell Wakefield in the English back row in 1920. Wakefield had stayed on in the R.A.F. and helped form its Rugby Union after the war. His impact for England was felt, almost literally, at once. Wakefield transformed forward play. Instead of continuing the with static, heaving scrums which had characterised the game before the war, he introduced a much more lively approach, attacking the opposing half-backs and linking up with three-quarter attacks. Soon this approach was being taken up by other nations as well.

Wakefield was also instrumental in improving the jumping in lineouts. He went on to become a Member of Parliament and the first Baron Wakefield of Kendal. A natural leader, in the same season he had captained the R.A.F. and Cambridge, where he had been on a course, and led the pack for England.

Accompanying Wakefield in the English back row of the time was a marauding open side flanker called Tommy Voyce. A man who usually played with a smile on his face, he was known to his fans as the Happy Warrior and to his opponents as the Grinning Menace. Dynamic about the field, his detractors claimed that he only pushed his weight in the pack in front of the selectors. His success was made all the more remarkable because he had lost most of the sight of one eye during the war.

By 1930, the selectors were beginning to show signs of initiative and make more use of modern technology. When the English hooker fell ill on the morning of the match against Wales at Twickenham, a replacement, Sam

# IN AND OUT

RIGHT Five Nations tournament match France v Scotland, 1931

Tucker, was flown to the ground from Bristol in a hired aeroplane, arriving just in time. The aircraft circled the ground to indicate the arrival of the player and then landed nearby, allowing Tucker to hurry over to the stadium. Completely unflustered, he performed so well that he was later made captain.

France continued to experience a miserable time in the Five Nations. It lost match after match and in one game suffered the ignominy of the referee calling the President of the French Rugby Union on to the field and ordering him to warn his players about their rough play. In 1920, it was defeated by Wales. In this game Jock Wemyss was recalled for Scotland. He was another international who had lost an eye in the war. When he had the temerity to ask for an international jersey in which to play he was told curtly that he had been given one six years earlier.

Wales had experienced a marvellous run. For twenty years between 1902 and 1922, discounting the war years it had won six championships and were runners up on seven occasions. Changes in the national economy were drastically to change this. On the whole, Welsh rugby suffered badly in the 1920s. In the great depression of the time, more than half a million people left in search of work elsewhere. Those rugby players who could, secured contracts with Rugby League sides, further weakening the national Union team.

The Five Nations was introduced to an even wider audience in 1927, when the Ireland-Scotland match became the subject of the first radio commentary. Several years earlier there had been two other significant milestones for Scotland. Murrayfield had hosted its first international and Scotland had won its first Grand Slam. In the following year it became the first Home Nations side to defeat England at Twickenham.

1928 saw Scotland adopt for the first time the practice of numbering the jerseys worn by its players, in a game against France. Afterwards members of the team were asked for their opinions on the innovation. Their response was so emphatically in the negative that the policy was rescinded. Not long afterwards at an international involving Scotland, King George V asked a senior Scottish administrator why the players bore no identifying marks on their shirts. He was informed frostily

that they were supposed to be watching a rugby match, not a cattle sale. Not until 1933 did the Scottish authorities give way to public opinion and allow numbered jerseys to be worn again by its players.

The organising unions of all the home countries continued to keep an almost neurotic eye open for transgressions against their code. In 1924, a

Welsh player, Ossie Male, boarded a train at Cardiff to travel to London and represent his country against England. He was sent straight home again from Paddington station because the administrators had discovered that he had played for his club the previous week, thus breaking the law that all selected representatives had to abstain from playing for at least six days before an international.

There was one bright period for France when it won a silver medal at the 1924 Olympics, but such an honour, against admittedly negligible opposition, was lightly regarded by the other members of the Five Nations. Only three teams entered and France was defeated in the final 17-3 by the U.S.A. The Americans may have been fired up by the fact that their dressing room had been broken into at a training possession and most of their clothes and possessions had been stolen.

Back in the Five Nations tournament the I.R.F.B. continued to worry about the indiscipline among the French players. There were lurid newspaper reports that they were even secreting knives in their stockings in case they had to defend themselves on the field.

An even more serious allegation as far as the authorities were concerned was that the French players were being paid for their efforts.

In 1931, ten French clubs broke away from their federation to form their own association. Fearing that this was going to lead to blatant professionalism the I.R.F.B. suspended France 'until we are satisfied that the control and conduct of the game has been placed on a satisfactory basis in all its essentials.' On 6th April 1931, in a defiant farewell, France beat England by 14 points to 13 at Stade Colombes. It was to be another 16 years before the home country played another championship game.

# What Did They Say?

*'Take a good look at it, boys, it's the last time any of you will see it at the expense of the Welsh Union!'*

**T.D. Schofield, Welsh Rugby official as his team passed the Forth Bridge the day after Wales had lost 35-10 to Scotland in 1924.**

# Chapter 3

# Back to Basics (1932-1946)

FREED FROM THE RESTRAINTS OF top class rugby, France started to play against such lesser nations as Germany and Romania and immediately won ten matches in a row. Back among the remaining championship sides matters were not so rosy. In 1932, all four of them lost to the touring South African side, which cast a shadow over the whole competition during that first year of what was now known as the Home Nations.

The South Africans had impressed everyone with their tactical use of kicking to touch, and this soon was to become a feature of international competition. Known as ten-man rugby the basic tactics consisted of the forwards winning the ball and the half-backs gaining ground by kicking for the line. Unfortunately this approach also led to a great deal of stultifying defensive play and the 1930s became notorious for its lacklustre international displays.

Another undeniable contributing factor to the comparative dullness of the decade was the fact that the former whipping-boy France was no longer around to ship points and boost the aggregates of the other nations. This was soon reflected in the paucity of tries scored in the new Four Nations format. Play also became increasingly negative, with fast breakaway forwards charged with harassing the opposing half-backs, thus breaking up the continuity and leading to further barren periods on the field.

The Home Nations championship up until the outbreak of war was a messy and indeterminate one, with no single nation establishing a commanding position. Between 1933 and 1939, Scotland, England and Ireland each won

**RIGHT** England
supporters tie colours
to the goalposts

# BACK TO BASICS

the championship twice. It was a sign of the lack of sparkle to the competition that in 1937 England was able to win the Triple Crown while scoring a total of only 19 points and conceding 14. Wales came out top once, in 1936.

All the Home Counties unions continued their united policy of parsimony. The English R.F.U. ordered all international shirts to be returned after a game. The official letter of selection from the official concerned always included the sentence 'A jersey will be provided to you, and must be returned to me directly after the game.' It was not long before the players were foiling this policy by promptly exchanging shirts with the opposing side at the final whistle.

The Scottish R.F.U. was so notorious for its meanness that when the coach driver dropped the side at the wrong gate for a Twickenham game and the players had to stroll round the ground to get to the changing rooms, sympathetic onlookers enquired if it was the latest economy of the association to make them walk from Scotland.

Reflecting the low-key ambience of the season, England, Ireland and Wales shared the championship in 1932. This was the season in which a change to the laws outlawed the practice of just two men in the front row and replacing these with three forwards, although this had been the practice in Home Countries sides for some time. One law, which was not repealed for a few years, was the one that allowed a side to choose either a throw-in or a scrum after a touch kick. Scotland, with a powerful pack, was noted for opting for the latter.

In the following year Wales pulled off a coup by defeating England at Twickenham for the first time, fielding seven new caps, although they lost their other two matches that season. Wales made a number of important changes for the game. Tired of losing so many players to premature retirements and the lure of Rugby League, the selectors abandoned their policy of going to the nearest pithead and whistling up a scrum half and three forwards.

Instead they started recruiting from public schools and universities. They started with a schoolboy and two undergraduates all of whom were later to play cricket for Glamorgan. There was a centre from Rydal School called Wilf Wooller, who went on to play for his country 18 times, survive a period in

# BACK TO BASICS

RIGHT Vivian Jenkins, the Welsh Rugby international, discussing rugby tactics

the notorious Changi prisoner of war camp in the Far East and return to captain Glamorgan at cricket. Next they brought in Vivian Jenkins a centre-turned-full-back from Oxford, and Maurice Turnbull, a cricketer and hockey player from Cambridge who had missed his rugby Blue but still turned out to be a useful scrum-half. Eleven years later he was to be killed by a sniper while serving with the Welsh Guards in Normandy.

The Ireland-Scotland match in 1933 was a particularly trying one for the Scottish players. Due to the terrible weather conditions the ship carrying them was unable to enter the shelter of Dublin Bay for 16 hours. When the players did finally stagger ashore they were in no state to play. Fortunately for them the pitch was in such a dreadful condition due to the blizzard that the game was postponed.

Scotland also defeated England by an unconverted try that year, although part of its victory was due to the fact that both of the English centres pulled up lame. Scotland went on to win the Triple Crown, a fitting farewell for its captain Ian Smith, 'the Flying Scot'.

Born in Melbourne and brought up in New Zealand, Smith had been educated in England and qualified for Scotland by virtue of his ancestry. He first played for Scotland in 1924, was a member of the Grand Slam-winning side of 1925, and scored a record-breaking 24 tries in 32 internationals.

England, during this period, set aside its usual Oxbridge bias and selected R. Leyland and J. Heaton, two centres who had honed their rugby skills at Liverpool University before going on to play for Lancashire.

Like Ian Smith, H.G. 'Tuppy' Owen-Smith was not born in the land he represented at rugby, but also became one of its most celebrated players of the time. He was a South African who played in five cricket Tests for the country of his birth in 1929, with a batting average of 42 runs. He attracted the attention of the English Rugby selectors as an attacking full-back for Cambridge University and as a result was capped ten times between 1934 and 1937, captaining the side in its championship and Triple Crown-winning side of 1937.

In the previous year another overseas-born player, a Russian prince studying at Oxford, had attracted notice by representing England four times.

LEFT Russian Prince Alexander Obolensky

Prince Alex Obolensky, the son of a White Russian officer who had fled with his family to Muswell Hill after the Russian Revolution, was surprisingly selected to play against the touring All Blacks. He scored two spectacular tries in an unprecedented 13-0 victory and retained his place for the Four Nations matches against Wales, Ireland and Scotland but, with poor service from his own side and being closely marked by opposing wingers, did not score again. Reputed to breakfast off oysters and champagne, Obolensky joined the R.A.F. as a pilot officer upon the outbreak of war but was killed at the age of 24 in a training crash while attempting a landing.

By now, international refereeing was generally of the highest standard, although there was one unusual officiating incident in a game between England and Wales at Twickenham. Wales were ahead 7-3 after a try had been scored. The conversion was narrowly missed, but the Welsh touch judge put up his flag to indicate a successful kick, while his English counterpart did not; neither did the referee whistle. Nevertheless, for the remainder of the match the scoreboard showed that the

**LEFT** England's Alex
Obolensky holds off
Scotland's Kenneth Fyfe

score was now 9-3 to Wales. Afterwards this was once again amended to 7-3.

Despite the victory the Welsh authorities were still worried. The experiment of trying to merge university players with hardened miners and labourers from the clubs was not working out particularly smoothly and there was much mutual animosity within the side.

On the international front there were problems with the Irish flag. The Ireland team comprised players from both the Republic of Ireland and Northern Ireland. In an effort to effect a compromise, the Irish Rugby Union

devised its own flag in 1925. After much prolonged debate, the I.R.F.B. decreed in 1932 that hitherto at Dublin's Lansdowne Road ground the Irish flag would have to be flown in conjunction with the I.R.U. one. At all other venues outside the Republic just the I.R.U. flag would be displayed.

Crowd control became an issue at the Wales-Ireland game at Cardiff Arms Park in 1936. Most tickets were available at the turnstiles and thousands queued for hours and then poured into the ground and onto the field. Match referee Cyril Gadney managed to reach one of the gates but when he told the

**ABOVE** The Irish
rugby team

custodian who he was he was at first refused admission because at least three others that morning had claimed to be in charge of the match.

Finally the gates were closed but were then rushed by thousands still outside the stadium, who also climbed over the high walls. Some fell and were

trampled on. Panic-stricken authorities ordered the Cardiff Fire Brigade to turns its hoses on the crowd, to little avail. The hosepipe incident was considered slightly counter-productive, as earlier in the day the ground authorities had spent considerable time and effort clearing the pitch of water. Eventually the game started but had to be halted on a number of occasions when spectators surged onto the pitch. Wingers taking throw-ins to the lineouts had to struggle for elbow-room, and some of the loose mauls ended up among the enthusiastic crowd. Wales won the game by three points to nil and became that year's champions.

With war approaching, the Home Countries made overtures to France once again, inviting them to return to the fold if their domestic game was now in order. There was some thought that the invitation was more of an attempt to offer solidarity across the Channel in the face of the impending conflict. In any event the French assured the I.R.F.B. that it now had professionalism under control, and they were invited to compete in the 1939-40 season. It was only a token gesture. There was to be no more competition, either at the Four Nations or Five Nations level for a number of years.

As had been the case in the First World War, thousands of athletes enlisted in the armed forces, and many did not return. A number of former rugby internationals were to lose their lives in the conflict, including 15 from Scotland, 14 from England, eight from France, seven from Ireland and three from Wales.

Wales, Ireland and England each won two matches in the final season, with Wales taking the championship by dint of a slightly superior points aggregate. It was a sign of the flatness of the season, and perhaps of the era, that only ten tries were scored in the whole championship that season. England was responsible for just one of them.

# What Did They Say?

*'Just give me my bus fare!'*

**Arsenal inside-forward Dr. Kevin O'Flanagan when asked by manager Tom Whittaker how much in the way of 'expenses' he wanted to play in a match for the First Division side. O'Flanagan represented Ireland at both soccer and rugby in the 1940s and was anxious to maintain his amateur status.**

# Chapter 4

# Post War (1947-1968)

ALTHOUGH THE FOUR NATIONS tournament was suspended during the war, a number of quasi-internationals were played during this period, including services matches and the unofficial 'Victory' matches of 1946. Many of the top pre-war players who survived the conflict, however, had been in action and had played little or no rugby.

When the new Five Nations competition started in 1947, at first the selectors had great difficulty in putting together efficient teams. Most of their initial selections contained a blend of experienced former internationals, some of whom had been absent for seven years, and new and raw up-and-coming players. England won the first post-war competition, losing only to Ireland, but it was the latter nation that was to emerge as the great side of the 1940s, heading the championship in 1948, 1949 and 1951.

England seemed oddly lacking in self-confidence. In the 1954 season it threw away leads against Ireland and France to secure a draw and a loss respectively. Two years later England, with ten players fresh to the international scene, lost 8-3 to Wales in a match that was to prove a baptism of fire for fly-half M.J.K. Smith of Oxford University, who won his only cap in this torrid game. Several years later he was to make up for this by gaining the first of his 50 cricket caps for England.

England still finished runners-up in this season and the newly appointed highly motivational captain, Eric Evans, regrouped and gathered around him the sturdiest of forwards in prop, Ron Jacobs, and the towering locks, David Marques and John Currie, who became so established that they were universally referred to in the same breath, like bacon and eggs. Before their international careers they had opposed each other four times in the annual Oxford-Cambridge matches.

Outside the pack, class was added to the side by the flying Coventry wing, Peter Jackson, who was never content to wait on the touchline but constantly came inside looking for the ball. At scrum-half, Dickie Jeeps played four times for the Lions before his country recognised his defensive capabilities and selected him. The reconstituted side was to win the Grand Slam in 1957, for the first time since 1928, and

**LEFT** Post war rugby boots

# POST WAR

RIGHT Eric Evans

the championship the year after. In 1960, England shared the championship with France, thanks mainly to the elusive running of newly arrived mercurial fly-half, Richard Sharp, from Oxford University.

The fly-half position had previously been occupied by Bev Risman, of whom much had been expected, but he caught the flu and was replaced by Sharp, who played superbly. Pragmatically Risman accepted the inevitable and transferred his considerable talents to Rugby League.

Ireland owed much of its considerable success during this period to the tactical genius of Jackie Kyle at half-back, and the leadership of its hooker, Karl Mullen, both of whom were medical students. Mullen took his chance when the Irish skipper was dropped in his favour. Later Ireland had a great result at Twickenham in 1964, when it defeated England 18-5. The Irish team contained some of its best-ever players in Mike Gibson, who played in four different positions for his country, full-back Tom Kiernan, who was in the losing side in all four matches in his initial Five Nations season, and boisterous lock-forward Willie John McBride.

Wales came back in 1952 to take the Grand Slam, with fly-half Cliff Morgan, who had made his international debut in the previous season, emerging as one of the greatest of all rugby half-backs, with a shrewd tactical brain and great acceleration. He was given his first international opportunity when Roy Burnett broke his collar-bone in a club match, leaving the Wales fly-half berth open. Morgan seized his opportunity and was to go on to win 29 caps for his country before retiring early at the age of 28. Wales also won the championship in 1956, yielding to England's Triple Crown and Grand Slam in 1957 and championship in the year after. On the other hand, Scotland suffered 17 successive defeats between 1951 and 1955.

The laws were still being tinkered with. During a game between Wales and England, Kevin Coslett, winning his first cap for England, took so long over his goal-kicks in a dull 0-0 match that afterwards the authorities decreed that a maximum of 60 seconds would be permitted for these operations. In a Wales-Scotland match, to secure a narrow victory, the Welsh exploited the standing rule that touch-kicks could then be taken from any part of the pitch to such an extent that the ball seemed to be out of play as often as it was in, leading to the law being changed later.

For most of this post-war period France had been hovering between mid-table respectability and the Wooden Spoon, although it did share the championship in 1954, forty years since it had first joined the Five Nations tournament. This was despite the fact that in back-row forward, Jean Prat, it had one of the most brilliant and charismatic players of the era. In 1955, he dropped two goals at Twickenham against England, a record for a forward. So highly was he regarded by opposition players, that at the end of his last Five Nations international, the 1955 France-Wales game in Paris, the Welsh players carried him off the pitch on their shoulders before a crowd of 75,000.

Off the field, France had only narrowly averted being banned from the tournament again in the early 1950s when the I.R.F.B. took exception to examples of professionalism among French clubs. For a time it looked as if the French Federation might even have to disband its club system, but this was avoided, and the country clung grimly on to its official international status.

**LEFT** Junior Springboks player Brian Harrison tries to prevent Dickie Jeeps kicking the ball during a game, 1962

# POST WAR

RIGHT RIGHT Irish rubgy player Karl Mullen tying his boot laces

Strangely enough, the French Rugby Union had actually profited from the war. In 1941, the Vichy French puppet government had declared that Rugby League was an unethical sport and had banned it, leaving Rugby Union to flourish.

In the 1950s and early 1960s, Gallic Rugby football entered a purple patch, when France threw off its rugby Cinderella image and emerged as one of the strongest nations.

It shared the title with England and Wales in 1954 and with Wales in the following year, before winning the championship outright in 1959. It then divided the championship with England in 1960 and then came out top on its own again in 1961 and 1962.

Much of the French success was due to a deep-thinking second-row forward, Lucien Mias, a teacher turned medical student. So revolutionary were his forward methods that he became known as Dr Pack. Mias was largely responsible for developing a group of big, tough, disciplined and above all, mobile forwards, capable of linking up with the backs in the loose. His team cut a swathe through the opposition for the best part of eight years.

Wales then had a good run at the

championship, sharing it with Scotland in 1964 and winning it outright, together with the Triple Crown, in 1966. In 1967, Wales appointed its first national coach, David Nash, who had a mixed start to his brief career. That season Wales took the Wooden Spoon, winning only one game, but that match was against England, in a 34-21 victory. Hero of the occasion was debutant full-back, Keith Jarrett, a recent school-leaver, who had never even visited Cardiff Arms Park as a spectator, let alone a player. Playing out of his normal club position he scored

RIGHT Frenchman Amedee Domenech playing a Five Nations tournament against England, 1962

a record-equalling 19 points there that afternoon. His total included a dazzling try from his own half of the field, during which he beat four would-be tacklers to touch the ball down in a corner. By so doing he prevented England from winning the Triple Crown that season, and let France in.

It was reputed that when Jarrett returned home to Newport late at night after his epic display, he was the only passenger on board a single-decker bus leaving the depot. A patriotic Welsh inspector ordered 'Get a double-decker for Mr Jarrett; he may want to go upstairs to smoke!' The youngster was soon on his way to professional Rugby League and presumably away from public transport. In 1967, another Welsh star, David Watkins, who had taken Cliff Morgan's place in the Wales team, also went north, this time for a record signing on fee reputed to be in the region of £15,000. David Nash, the Wales coach, did not have such a rewarding time. At the end of the season the Welsh Union decided not to take him on the country's tour of New Zealand, effectively ending his time in charge.

Towards the end of the period

England had an undistinguished record and had to be content with securing mere crumbs from the rugby table. One of the more nourishing of these was glimpsed in a Calcutta Cup match against Scotland in 1965, when both countries occupied the bottom positions in the championship. In an otherwise dull match, in injury time England winger, Andy Hancock, picked up the ball in his own half and ran 85 yards to score what was immortalised as 'Hancock's Try', and secure a last-minute draw for his country.

# What Did They Say?

*'Excuse me, has anyone got some hairy twine for my boots?'*

**Tony O'Reilly, Irish winger, wandering into the England dressing-room before the match against England at Twickenham in 1956, in search of a lost bootlace, and interrupting the flow of captain Eric Evans' fiery pre-match peroration to the England players.**

# Chapter 5

# Years of the Dragon (1969-1980)

FRANCE CONTINUED TO BE A RUgby presence throughout the 1970s, but this was undoubtedly the decade of Wales as the pre-eminent Five Nations force. Between 1969 and 1979 it won the Five Nations championship five times, the Triple Crown five times and the Grand Slam three times. It won nine out of ten games against England and eight out of ten against Scotland. Between 1964 and 1979 Wales lost only once to England, a run of 16 matches.

The real impetus for this resurgence was probably due to a humiliating defeat at the hands of South Africa in Durban in 1964. After this the Welsh National Union made a determined effort to revive Wales' rugby fortunes.

In 1968, a national coach was appointed. Improved facilities and organisation coincided with the arrival of a host of talented younger players who were soon to dominate the game. Welsh coaching methods revolutionised rugby. The execution of these methods on the pitch made the game as exciting as it had ever been.

In 1967, Gareth Edwards, the son of a miner, made his international debut as scrum-half, displaying a searing service from the scrum, a scintillating break and an increasingly effective long rolling kick to touch. Two years later, at the age of 20, he was Wales' youngest ever captain.

He joined fly-half Barry John, who

had made an uncertain international start, but then burst into amazing life with his improvisational skills and apparently effortless control of a game. His international tenure was a relatively short one. 'The King' retired at his peak at the age of 27, unable to reconcile the pressures of being a sporting idol with holding down an ordinary job for the rest of the week. John claimed that he was tired of living in a goldfish bowl.

Phil Bennett had been playing for Wales in a number of positions since 1969, but it was not until the retirement of John in 1971 that Bennett made the fly-half spot his own. With his evasive running and superb kicking he had a claim to being his era's most complete player.

At Millfield School, Gareth Edwards had played alongside J.P.R. Williams. They met up again for Wales, when Williams was a 19-year-old medical student who was to play 55 times for his country as an almost unbelievably brave attacking full-back, his flying mane of hair often surmounting a bleeding face and once, against Scotland in 1972, a broken jaw. He was also versatile enough to play with gusto for his country in the back row of the scrum on an

LEFT The great fly-half Barry John

RIGHT John Dawes is carried on the shoulders of Gareth Edwards, as Wales celebrate their Five Nations victory, 1971

injury-beset tour of Australia. With Gerald Davies and Ray Gravell and a pack headed by the ball-winning Mervyn Davies at number eight, they made a team born to dominate, which is just what Wales did for some seasons.

They were supervised by two very different coaches. Clive Rowlands, a former scrum-half and captain of Pontypool, Swansea and Wales, was in charge for 28 games between 1968 and 1974, winning 18 and drawing seven of them, before giving way to John Dawes, who had played under Rowlands for Wales in the centre. Dawes continued in the post until 1979, winning 18 out of 24 internationals played. Rowlands recognised the talent under his command, introduced squad training but allowed the players time to settle in and encouraged them to express themselves on the field to the full. John Dawes was a tactical genius with the rare ability to put his theories into practice. He had first attracted favourable notice with his methods at the London Welsh club, turning the side into a breathtakingly attacking unit. During his playing days he had had his own troubles with the whims of selectors because of his indi-

viduality and perceived lack of pace. This made him receptive and sympathetic to the problems of the gifted players around him.

The games Wales played during this season were usually executed with considerable flair and style, together with the occasional dramatic climax. Against Scotland at Murrayfield in 1971 everything hinged on a kick from the right-hand touchline by the left-footed London Welsh wing-forward John Taylor. He succeeded, to give Wales a 19-18 victory and the credit for having pulled off, as one newspaper termed it, 'the greatest conversion since St Paul!' So popular did the side become that against Scotland at Murrayfield in 1975, the largest crowd ever to watch a rugby match, 104,000, turned up to see Wales go down to a rare defeat, 12-10.

Despite the occasional loss, for almost a decade Wales softened up opposing packs and then ruthlessly cut through defences. The team's peak period coincided with a significant change to the scoring system, with the number of points for a try increased from three to four, encouraging attacking play.

To reinforce its glittering array of stars, Wales could also produce the soli-

tary man for the big occasion and be dispassionate in disposing of him afterwards. There were two examples of this in a single season in 1970. In the Scotland match Newport's Laurie Daniel scored a try and converted one, but never played for his country again. Three weeks later against England at Twickenham, Chico Hopkins came off the bench for his only cap, after a sojourn of almost 20 matches on the sidelines. With Wales trailing 6-13, he made one try and scored another to secure victory for his country before disappearing into the northern regions of Rugby League.

Wales' superiority was emphasised by the number of points it was able to amass against the other Five Nations sides during this period. Hardly a season went by without at least one impressive compilation: 23 against Ireland in 1970, 35 against Scotland in 1972, 25 against England in1973, 25 against France in 1975, 28 against Scotland in 1976 and 27 against England in 1979. One of its strangest victories was a 28-6 win over Wales at Cardiff in 1976. Towards the end of the game the French referee pulled a muscle and injured his leg but refused to be replaced, hobbling dramatically but to little purpose some yards behind the play for the last part of the game, ignoring the offer of a touch-judge to replace him and manifestly failing to secure the sympathy vote from the exasperated crowd.

The all-conquering side was broken up in the mid-1970s, but was reassembled almost immediately, this time with the titanic front-row trio of Charlie Faulkner, Bobby Windsor and Graham Price to win the ball and terrorise opponents.

One slightly fortuitous victory was gained over Ireland in 1979 at Cardiff Arms Park. Ireland had been eking out a narrow lead when the Irish full-back Dick Spring dropped the ball. A Welsh player gathered it and scored, giving Wales 24-21 victory. Spring, who had been a Manhattan bartender and was to go on to become his country's Deputy Prime Minister and Foreign Minister, was convinced at the time that his budding political career was over. 'I would have found it easier to have been adopted by a Welsh constituency than an Irish one after I dropped that ball,' he said feelingly.

Despite its record of wins, Wales did

not have it all completely its own way during this period. In the 1970s, France won the championship twice, and Scotland, Ireland and England either won or shared the Five Nations title once. In 1973 there was a five-way tie for the championship, with each team winning and losing two games. However,

developed in the first era, relying on a massive, fast pack. Three prominent members of that scrum, Rives, Palmie and Vaquerin went on to very different futures. The blond Jean-Pierre Rives was the outstanding flanker of his time, with 59 caps. After his retirement he became a successful sculptor and Seine-side restaurant owner. Michel Palmie was banned from rugby after permanently impairing the sight of an opponent with a punch in a club game in 1978. Prop Armand Vaquerin died in 1980 after playing Russian Roulette in a French bar.

The unluckiest French player in this period was Jean-Pierre Salut, who tripped while running out of the changing room at Stade de Colombes before a game against Scotland and broke his leg before he could even get on to the field. The Grand Slam was won in 1977 with the same 15 men playing in each of the four games, without conceding a single try. The 1972 championship was not completed, because Scotland and Wales refused to play Ireland in Dublin, in view of the possible dangers of the political situation after an attack on the British Embassy in the Irish capital. England did travel, only to lose, giving rise to captain John Pullen's trenchant

Scotland had scored many more points than the other nations and so was awarded its first title for 27 years.

France maintained its brand of rugby

**RIGHT** Jean-Pierre
Rives of France became
his country's most
capped flanker

and enthusiastically applauded post-match remark, 'We may not be very good, but at least we turn up!'

Ireland was going through one of its increasing happy-go-lucky but ineffectual phases, as exemplified by forward Willy Duggan's dictum that training blunted a player's cutting edge. Throughout the 1970s and for some time after, Ireland's rugby became more famed for a number of possibly apocryphal stories than for its on-field successes. In an effort to reverse its fortunes it recalled charismatic winger Tony O'Reilly after a seven-year absence for a game against England at Twickenham. By this time the winger was a successful businessman and turned up at the ground in a chauffeur-driven limousine, a fact not unnoticed by the fans. In the course of the game, won 9-3 by England, O'Reilly found himself subjected to the attention of English boots when he fell bravely on the ball. A roar of approbation for his assailants went up from the crowd, followed by a piercing cry of 'Well done! Now go and kick his chauffeur!'

England generally had a poor decade, taking four Wooden Spoons, while Scotland accumulated three. The era began on a low note when the unfeeling selectors picked full-back Bob Hillier as captain for all five internationals in the 1969-70 season and then dropped him cursorily after three. Conversely, England did well outside the Five Nations tournament. Between 1972 and 1973, after losing half a dozen internationals in a row, it defeated South Africa, New Zealand and Australia. Normal service was then resumed when the country went on to lose nine of its next eleven matches.

# What Did They Say?

*'When we packed down, I'd hear him say, '"Bob-bee. Bob-bee" and then his big fist would come through and smack you in the chops. To get my own back I booted him in the mush as hard as I could. He got up and gave me a wink.'*

**Wales hooker Bobby Windsor recounting his on-field international encounters with French player Alan Esteve, 'the Beast Of Belziers', in the 1970s.**

# Chapter 6

# England Emerges – Briefly (1981-1999)

IN 1980, ENGLAND EMERGED FROM the doldrums to win the Grand Slam for the first time in 23 years. The side was given impetus by the result of a game played earlier in the year, when the North of England side had pulled off a shock success by defeating the touring All Blacks, with hooker Stevie Smith and winger Mike Slemen playing particularly well. Consequently, the England side selected for that season was constructed around the Northern players, led by burly second-row forward Bill Beaumont of the Fylde club. A last minute replacement due to injury was centre Clive Woodward, who brought added creativity to the speed already present among the backs.

The England game plan was based on keeping the ball tight among the forwards, or sticking it up their jumpers as the more jaundiced spectators sometimes termed it. This approach was noted although not necessarily approved of by the young Woodward, who later would return to the England set-up in another and more influential guise.

In the first match of the season, England recovered from being 9-3 down against Ireland to win, and then went on to defeat France in Paris. Next they came up against Wales in the so-called 'Battle of Twickenham'. After a bloody and often dirty match England won by a penalty from full-back Dusty Hare in the closing moments. Wales had played a man short for most of the game after Paul Ringer had been sent off for a late tackle 14 minutes into the game.

Afterwards, in a burst of self-pity, the excluded Ringer complained darkly, 'People have been inventing things about me ever since I was said to have shot a cow in Brecon.' Rod Morgan, manager of the team blamed the Ringer sending off for the following period of Welsh decline, complaining that the incident had taken all the fire out of his

LEFT Bill Beaumont runs with ball during the Five Nations match against Scotland, 1980

blow in 1982, when Bill Beaumont had to retire from rugby due to a bad head injury. His retirement coincided with those of several other members of the once all-powerful pack, including Utley. For the next twenty years all the Five Nations teams jostled for supremacy and each one had its moments of triumph. France won the Grand Slam in 1981, shared the title with Ireland several seasons later, divided it again with Scotland in 1986 and with Wales two years after that. Before the end of the century it had topped the table again on four more occasions, including two more Grand Slams. Driven on by the dynamic Jean-Pierre Rives, the closely-knit side was a considerable force.

Continuity for the next great generation of French rugby players was provided in 1980 by the arrival of the brilliant, Venezuelan-born, attacking full-back Serge Blanco, who went on to play 93 times for his country, despite his habit of smoking 20 cigarettes a day. Throughout the decade, France continued to play champagne rugby. When Philippe Sella scored a try against Ireland in Paris in 1986, the ball had been passed more than 20 consecutive times.

side. With Beaumont and Roger Utley in the English pack, fans anticipated a further run of success over the next few seasons, but almost immediately England slipped back to mid-table mediocrity. The team suffered a major

Ireland, as usual, continued to produce talented individual players, although they did not always jell as a team. They got it right with a vengeance in the early 1980s, however, winning the championship outright in 1982 and 1985, and sharing it in 1983. The 1982 title, secured under the captaincy of army officer Ciaran Fitzgerald, was Ireland's first championship for 23 years. During this period the country's rugby fans witnessed a gritty struggle for the fly-half position between two supremely talented players, Tony Ward and Olly Campbell. Campbell, an intellectual, scheming half-back was generally preferred by the selectors to Ward, a flair player. He justified his selection by amassing 217 points for his country in 22 appearances between 1976 and 1984.

The golden age of the 1970s had come to an end for Wales, but it still managed to tie for the championship once and win it outright on another occasion. Gareth Edwards had been succeeded at scrum-half by another fine prospect in Terry Holmes, who played for his country for seven years. In 1985, disillusioned by Wales' lack of success he opted for a Rugby League career, signing for Bradford Northern, for

£80,000. Always injury-prone, Holmes played only 40 games as a professional before being forced to retire.

Wales' great player of the 1980s and early 1990s, however, was fly-half Jonathan Davies, a scintillating half-back who also transferred his skills to Rugby League, with more success than Holmes. Like Holmes, he was often playing in a poor national side and his efforts to suggest changes were ignored by the authorities, making him as disillusioned with the situation as Holmes had been. He accepted a fee of £225,000 to play professionally, although he did return to play a few Rugby Union games for his country again in the 1990s.

Scotland won the Grand Slam in 1984, shared the championship two years later and took the title outright in 1990 and 1999. The nation's emerging brand of distinctive play owed much to its coach, Jim Telfer, a former international player, who was appointed in 1980. Nine years earlier, greatly daring, the Scottish Rugby Union had appointed its first full-time head coach although it fell short of calling him this, preferring the title 'adviser to the captain.' Telfer's role was altogether more clearly defined. His arrival coincided

# ENGLAND EMERGES – BRIEFLY

with a period when Scottish clubs were beginning to develop their own high quality players and Telfer did not have to rely so much on exiled Scots playing south of the border.

The new coach put together the outstanding half-back partnership of John Rutherford and Roy Laidlaw and brought in back row players of the calibre of John Jeffrey and the twins, Jim and Finlay Calder. After several seasons of steady progress, in 1984 Scotland defeated Wales, England and Ireland with increasing confidence and then triumphed 21-12 over France, who also could have had a Grand Slam if it had won this final match. In the early 1980s, outside the Five Nations competition, Scotland also pulled off a victory against Australia and a draw with the All Blacks.

Two years later, in 1986, Scotland shared the title with France. Gavin Hastings made a successful debut at full-back by scoring all his team's 18 points in the match. After a defeat against Wales, Scotland went on to defeat England by a large margin, and then Ireland by one point.

England's bad patch continued. In the year in which Scotland and France had divided the championship between them, England had not won more than two matches in a season for four years. In 1983 it had lost three matches and drawn one out of four in the championship, and had ended up with the Wooden Spoon.

Things began to look up in 1986 with the arrival of one of the best number eight forwards to wear an England shirt. His name was Dean Richards. He was 22 years old and worked as a Leicestershire policeman. He was a huge, shambling man, weighing 18 stone, with enormous strength and a great sense of where the ball was going next. In his debut game against Ireland he revitalised the pack, scored two tries and should have had a third if the ball had not been hacked illegally out of his hands.

England lost its next game 33-6 to Scotland. This turned out to be something of a blessing in disguise, because the thrashing prompted the selectors to have a clearout of some of the existing players. Joining the newly arrived Richards were winger Rory Underwood and hooker Gareth Chilcott, whose versatile post-rugby career was to embrace appearances in pantomime. They, and a number of other emerging stars, were to

**ABOVE** James Doyle of Ireland (right) chases Lain Hunter (centre) of Scotland

**RIGHT** Scotland v England, 1987

bed in to the side comfortably and gain experience over the next few years.

For the England side of this time more seemed to be happening off the field than on it. The 1988 Calcutta Cup match was a dour affair, with England eking out a 9-5 victory. The post-match celebrations, on the other hand, were anything but dull. There were drunken altercations between the players and then in the small hours of the morning the erstwhile peacemakers Scottish flanker John Jeffrey and the England colossus at number eight Dean Richards wandered off with the precious over 100-years-old Calcutta Cup and decided to play rugby with it in Edinburgh's Princes Street, with the inevitable results. Richards was banned for one match for his part in the shenanigans, while to the wrath of Scottish supporters, Jeffrey was suspended for six months

Another off-field incident in the same

# ENGLAND EMERGES – BRIEFLY

year saw England adopting its unofficial national rugby song. During a period in which it had lost 15 out of 23 matches, in the last game of the season it was trailing 3-0 to Ireland at Twickenham. A second-half renaissance was sparked off by Chris Oti, who had made his debut earlier in the season and was the first black player to represent England for 80 years. He scored three out of six tries for his country to win the game 35-3. In honour of Oti's performance a group of students from Douai school in the crowd, started singing Sing Low, Sweet Chariot, a plantation spiritual and rugby club favourite. The whole crowd took up the refrain, which became a Twickenham standard. Oti played a few more games for England but was forced to retire though injury.

An embarrassing defeat to Wales in the quarter-final of the first Rugby World Cup led to Geoff Cooke being appointed the new England manager. Cooke was one of the country's leading rugby thinkers. His own playing career had only been conducted at club and county level, but he had been an outstanding coach and chairman of the England selectors panel. From the beginning he told his squad that they were going to have to think about their rugby as never before and achieve standards of fitness that some of them might not think possible.

Not all his players encompassed his viewpoint and were slow to study the videos and listen to the motivational tapes provided by the new backup team, and there were differences of opinion between some members of the squad and the newly appointed management. Cooke stuck to his guns, even to the extent of not selecting the enormously popular Dean Richards for the whole of one season because the closely-scrutinised number eight was not regarded as mobile enough throughout a game against Canada. Richards was however picked for the Lions during this period and eventually made his impressive and impassive way back into the Five Nations set-up.

Cooke's methods began to bear fruit. A fitter, better prepared England side started to string an impressive series of victories together, winning the championship and Grand Slam in 1991, 1992 and 1995, and the championship alone in 1996. The team was also runners-up in 1993. The year before that the value of a try had been increased to five points

# ENGLAND EMERGES – BRIEFLY

**RIGHT** Chris Oti celebrates with team mates during a match against Ireland, 1988

making some Five Nations victories by all the nations look more impressive than they might otherwise had done.

Throughout most of this period England had been captained by centre Will Carling. He had led the team from his first season as an international in 1988, presiding over a team of what seemed like all the talents, which included fly-half Rob Andrew and Carling's fellow centre Jeremy Guscott. It was a sign of Carling's popularity among the players, if not with the administrators, that when at one juncture, in an unguarded moment, he was threatened with dismissal for calling the members of the R.F.U. committee '57 old farts', none of the others would accept the captaincy, leading to his reinstatement, after an apology had been offered and accepted.

England had been on its way to another Grand Slam in 1990, under Carling, but fell at the final hurdle against Scotland, also undefeated that season, at Murrayfield. The highly successful England side was perceived as arrogant in some quarters, especially in Scotland. In one of the best stage-managed entrances ever seen in the Five Nations, instead of running on to the

field captain David Sole led the Scottish side out at a measured pace, to enormous acclaim. The Scots had fielded the same side for all four Five Nations games that season and it showed in their teamwork and understanding. In dreadful weather the side fought tenaciously, won 13-7 and took the Grand Slam, the third in its history.

The following season England recovered sufficiently to go on to win the championship four times in the 1990s, including two Grand Slams. In 1991 the team scored a record 118 points while winning the title. In the same year England reached the final of the World Cup, losing 12-6 to Australia. The next year was another Grand Slam for Carling's players. That season the biggest threat to its success occurred when Dean Richards got stuck temporarily in a lift on his way down to the pitch to substitute for Tim Rodber in the match against Scotland.

The following game, against France, saw two French players sent off in a violent match, which England won 31-13. The offenders were prop Gregoire Lescube and hooker Vincent Moscato. It came as no surprise to English supporters to learn that Moscato moonlighted

as a small-part villain in French gangster movies. Both of the banished French players were suspended for six months.

Despite its success, there were complaints that this was another unadven-

turous England side, over reliant on its forwards and content to grind out victories. Nevertheless, the team continued to win. Carling captained England until 1996 and continued to play for the side for some time after that.

In 1997, Clive Woodward, the former centre, became England's new coach. Early on in his reign he survived an embarrassing crushing 76-0 defeat to the Wallabies in Australia, in what was known as the 'tour from hell'. The new coach persevered. Patiently he started to assemble what was to become England's most successful rugby side. He presented each player with his own fitness and dietary programme. He had inherited a stupendous second-row forward in Martin Johnson and recruited a brilliant 18-year-old all-kicking all-tackling 18-year-old fly-half, Jonny Wilkinson, and a rock of a prop-forward called Jason Leonard, who was to gain over 100 caps. Slowly Woodward gained the trust and affection of his team. Martin Johnson said admiringly of the coach and his methods, 'Clive used to call himself the "Crazy Professor" and he wasn't far off.'

A hiccup occurred when Woodward's captain, number eight, Lawrence

**LEFT** England's 1995
Grand Slam team

# ENGLAND EMERGES – BRIEFLY

RIGHT **RIGHT** Fabien Pelous
and Oliver Roumat
celebrate an Adbel
Benazzi try

Dallaglio, was trapped by a national newspaper into claiming that he had taken drugs, a charge he subsequently denied, although he pleaded guilty to bringing the game into disrepute and stepped down from the side. He was too good a player to be left out for long and was later reinstated, although no longer as captain. England did not feature much in the championship during the closing years of the 20th century, but its day was soon to dawn.

France came back to win back-to-back Grand Slams in 1997 and 1998. Powered by forwards Abdel Benazzi and Rafael Ibanez they showed great resolution against England when winning the first of the two Grand Slams. At one stage France was losing 20-6, only to dig in and take the match 23-20. In the next year they beat Wales 51-0 on their way to a whitewash over the other nations.

While France had been rampant, Scotland had had a very poor season. In their two home matches they had conceded a total of 11 tries and in two years had won only one match at Murrayfield. Suddenly in the last year of the decade Scotland showed sparkling form to win the championship most unexpectedly, culminating by scoring

five tries against France. A cloud was cast over the victory by objections to a number of so-called 'Kilted Kiwis' appearing in the team. These included players like the Leslie brothers, John and Martin, and Glenn Metcalfe, all New

ABOVE Roger Uttley and Clive Woodward hold the English Rose during a press conference to announce the new England Coach, 1997

**ABOVE** Jonny Wilkinson during a Five Nations match, 1999

Zealanders with an occasional Scottish grandparent to be found on their family trees. At least one former Scottish international complained 'I don't think you can have five or six players with New Zealand accents in the Scottish team.'

Meanwhile, two great rugby changes had taken place in the last two decades of the 20th century. In 1987, the World Cup tournament had been inaugurated and eight years later professionalism had been introduced.

turn out for his country himself if need be. The situation was resolved. More serious problems were presented when in 1996 and 1999 England was ejected briefly from the next Five Nations tournament over disputes over the English R.F.U. signing separate contracts with Sky Television. In each case the English authorities climbed down and the nation was reinstated. The year 2000 was to see yet another innovation. The Five Nations became Six.

# What Did They Say?

*'Colin may not have looked so good, but I'm told he smelled lovely!'*

**England captain Steve Smith on prop-forward Colin Smart after the latter had been carried away to hospital after drinking a complimentary bottle of after-shave lotion during the post-match dinner after England's 27-15 victory over France at Parc des Princes, Paris, in February, 1982.**

The impact of so much money being poured into the game had its disadvantages. On one occasion when the England players threatened to strike over contract disputes an incensed Clive Woodward said that he would

# Chapter 7

# The Six Nations (2000-2008)

THE ARRIVAL OF THE NEW MILLennium also saw new challenges in the tournament. While England had been dithering about whether or not to reapply for admission to the Five Nations without losing too much face in 1999, preparations were being made behind the scenes to fast-forward Italy into the competition should the English drop out altogether. However, England soon resumed its place and Italy did not become a member of what would be renamed the Six Nations until the original planned date of 2000.

Rugby was introduced to Italy by English expatriates in the country towards the end of the 19th century. By 1929 there were 16 teams in the country and Italy had lost its first international, 9-0 to Spain. The sport received an impetus from Allied troops stationed in Italy after the Second World War and the national team progressed from challenging countries like Romania and Germany to higher grade matches against South Africa, Australia, New Zealand and England. Since 1980, the Italian Rugby Federation made determined attempts to be accepted into the Five Nations competition. Victories over Ireland in 1995 and France two years later helped to persuade the organisers to consider admitting Italy, although there were doubts that the latest member would be good enough.

For a brief time it looked as if these fears were unfounded when, in its first match in the 2000 tournament, Italy beat the previous season's championship winners Scotland. It was, however, to be some time before this victory could be duplicated against any of the other nations in the tournament and by

the end of the 2008 campaign the Italians had only registered six wins and one draw in 45 matches.

As it happened, Italy was not the only side to struggle over the next few seasons. France and England exerted such a stranglehold over the competition that newspapers began to wonder aloud whether the Six Nations was becoming too much of a two-horse race.

England, with the 2003 World Cup in its sights, began by taking the first two championships of the 21st century although in each season it lost crucial games (against Scotland in 2000 and Ireland a year later) to be denied both the Triple Crown and the Grand Slam. The 2001 schedule had been interrupted by an outbreak of foot and mouth disease amongst cattle in Britain, causing international matches against Ireland to be postponed and not played until the September and October.

In 2002, France won the Six Nations championship but England retained enough form to take the Triple Crown. The side peaked the following year, winning both the Grand Slam and the World Cup, with a 20-17 win over Australia, thanks to a famous last minute drop goal from Jonny Wilkinson.

LEFT Jason Robinson of England makes a break

## THE SIX NATIONS

Jason Robinson a former Rugby League player who had sparkled in the World Cup, took over the captaincy as Wilkinson then suffered a series of injuries. A dashing winger-cum-full-back, he was known as Billy Whizz for his incredible side-stepping sprints through the opposition.

Despite all Robinson's efforts, 2004 proved an anti-climax. The ageing side was beginning to break up and Clive Woodward was growing weary of the constant internecine strife between the R.F.U. and the major English clubs. England lost to France and Ireland and finished third in the championship, which was won by France. Woodward resigned to switch codes and take up a position with Southampton Football Club.

He was replaced by former England wing-forward Andy Robinson, whose tenure was brief and inglorious. Under his guidance, England finished fourth in the 2005 championship and lost 31-6 to France in Paris the following March, its biggest defeat for 20 years. By the end of the season, England had lost eight out of its last nine internationals and Robinson resigned to be replaced by Brian Ashton. For four years Ashton

**LEFT** Sebastien Chabal of France charges through the Irish defence, February 2007

form, England could not maintain this standard and finished third, behind France and Ireland.

The beginning of the 21st century may have belonged to England, but France was about to recover all its old exciting if inconsistent form. It had the same type of marauding forwards that had always brought it success. In this era they included the two exciting bruisers Raphael Ibanez and Sebastien Chabal, both of whom plied their trade in England, with Wasps and Sale respectively. In 1999, Bernard Laporte had been appointed the national head coach and the next seven years proved a rollercoaster ride for the followers of French rugby. Playing with flair and sometimes craziness, Laporte's initial season saw France win its first three matches and take second place in the championship behind England. The effort seemed to have exhausted the players because the side plummeted to fifth place the following season. 2002 and 2004, however, saw Laporte's side win Grand Slams, interspersed with a third place in 2003. In 2005, France was second, behind Wales, but then the next two years saw it topping the championship again before finishing third in 2008.

**ABOVE** Scotland's captain Chris Patterson (Left) is tackled by France's wing Vincent Clerc (Right) during the 2007 final

had been Woodward's assistant in the England set-up and started his first season in charge well with a good win in the Calcutta Cup over Scotland. True to

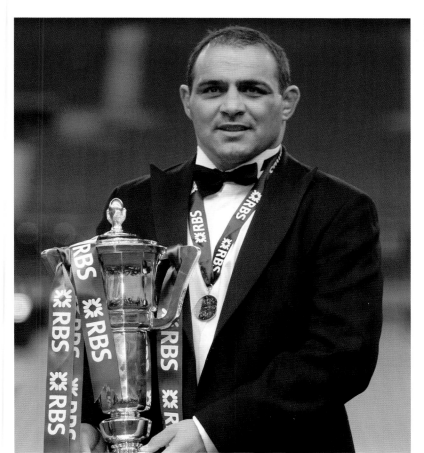

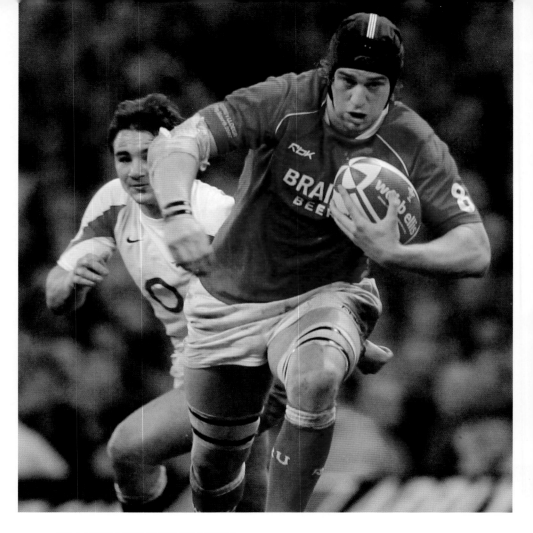

Only one nation broke the early 21st century Six Nations stranglehold exerted by France and England, and that was Wales in 2005 and 2008. For the first time in 27 years – since the glory days of the 1970s – it carried off the Grand Slam. The team started in great style by defeating England by two points at Twickenham, thanks to a last-minute 40-yard penalty from Gavin Henson, the spiky-haired new kid on the block. This was followed by a 38-8 victory over Italy in Rome. Wales next travelled to Paris and by half-time were 15-6 down in the face of some all-action flowing rugby by the home side. Two second-half tries by Martyn Williams put Wales back in contention and they won 24-18. The game against Scotland at Murrayfield saw a feast of tries and a final score of 46-22 in favour of the visitors. The last Six Nations game of the season was a home fixture at the Millennium against Ireland. Stephen Jones and Gavin Henson kicked magnificently to win the match and end a great season for Wales. The final score was 32-20 and there were raucous celebrations in the streets and pubs of Cardiff.

Sadly for their fans, Wales disap-peared into oblivion during the 2006 and 2007 seasons and, while there were some highlights such as a 27-18 victory over England in the final game to avoid the 2007 Wooden Spoon, there were plenty of lows. A controversial draw at home to Italy in March 2006 was fol-lowed a year later by another con-tentious match in Rome. With the clock ticking down, the Welsh players checked with referee Chris White that they had time to take another lineout but once the ball was kicked into touch the final whistle was blown and Italy celebrated a 23-20 victory.

Following a disappointing World Cup, Wales entered the fray in 2008 and quickly registered their first win at Twickenham for 20 years, followed by convincing triumphs over Scotland and Italy. A narrow 16-12 victory away to Ireland saw them claim the Triple Crown and a spirited performance at home to France gave them their second Grand Slam in four years while Shane Williams touched down to become his country's leading try scorer with 41.

The other Six Nations sides entered the 21st century with their enthusiasm unabated but found success hard to come by. Ireland, chasing their first

**LEFT** Action from the Wales v England match, one of their better games, 2007

ABOVE The Welsh
team celebrate winning
in 2008

championship since 1985 and their first
Grand Slam since 1948, managed to
claim the Triple Crown in 2004, 2006
and 2007 but could not find the ruthless
touch necessary to defeat all their opponents. They have, nevertheless, been the
second most successful nation in the
tournament (behind France) in the

2000s in terms of games won. Coach
Eddie O'Sullivan built a talented team
around Brian O'Driscoll and, while
some critics would argue that Ireland
relied too heavily on their talismanic
captain, the team has established a rep-
utation for playing entertaining rugby.
After a disappointing 2007 World Cup

and a dismal Six Nations showing the following year when the Irish – who played their home games at Croke Park while their traditional Lansdowne Road home was being redeveloped – finished a lowly fourth, O'Sullivan resigned and was replaced by Declan Kidney.

Scotland started the first day of the Six Nations tournament by losing 34-20 to Italy, Diego Dominguez scoring 29 points with the boot. After that matters did not greatly improve although they have beaten the Auld Enemy three times to claim the Calcutta Cup (2000, 2006 and 2008). In the first nine years of the Six Nations, Scotland has never finished higher than third. They have achieved this twice (2001 and 2006), as well as being fourth twice while they finished fifth on three occasions and have twice been the unwilling recipients of the Wooden Spoon. The period also included a 46-19 thrashing by France while February 2007 saw them become the first team to lose at home to Italy (37-17).

Newcomers Italy struggled for a long time. Their scrum was a mighty one but it was not matched by the technical skills of their backs. After their victory on the opening day of the 2000 Six Nations they had to wait until 2007 for their next wins (against Scotland and Wales), to leave them in an unprecedented fourth place in the championship, above the two nations they had defeated. Indeed, these two sides are the only Six Nations opponents the Azzurri have ever beaten but who can predict what will happen in the future?

Before the last round of the 2007 Six Nations competition, France, Ireland, England and Italy were, in theory, all in a position to win it. In the end France pulled away to become champions. It was a sign of how much time had passed and how many changes had been made since the first 19th century games. Now all the Six Nations teams have had their moments of glory.

# What Did They Say?

*'His hallmark was his inexhaustible search for that step ahead.'*

**Jonny Wilkinson on Sir Clive Woodward.**

**LEFT** Wales v France at the Millennium Stadium, 2008

# Appendix

# Championship Winners

| Date | Country |
|------|---------|
| 1883 | England |
| 1884 | England |
| 1885 | Not Completed |
| 1886 | England & Scotland |
| 1887 | Scotland |
| 1888-1889 | Not Completed |
| 1890 | England & Scotland |
| 1891 | Scotland |
| 1892 | England |
| 1893 | Wales |
| 1894 | Ireland |
| 1895 | Scotland |
| 1896 | Ireland |
| 1897-1898 | Not Completed |
| 1899 | Ireland |
| 1900 | Wales |
| 1901 | Scotland |
| 1902 | Wales |

| Date | Country |
|------|---------|
| 1903 | Scotland |
| 1904 | Scotland |
| 1905 | Wales |
| 1906 | Wales & Ireland |
| 1907 | Scotland |
| 1908 | Wales |
| 1909 | Wales |
| 1910 | England |
| 1911 | Wales |
| 1912 | England & Ireland |
| 1913 | England |
| 1914 | England |
| 1915-1919 | Not Held |
| 1920 | England, Scotland & Wales |
| 1921 | England |
| 1922 | Wales |
| 1923 | England |
| 1924 | England |

# CHAMPIONSHIP WINNERS

| Date | Country |
|------|---------|
| 1925 | Scotland |
| 1926 | Ireland & Scotland |
| 1927 | Ireland & Scotland |
| 1928 | England |
| 1929 | Scotland |
| 1930 | England |
| 1931 | Wales |
| 1932 | England, Ireland & Wales |
| 1933 | Scotland |
| 1934 | England |
| 1935 | Ireland |
| 1936 | Wales |
| 1937 | England |
| 1938 | Scotland |
| 1939 | England & Ireland & Wales |
| 1940-1946 | Not Held |
| 1947 | England & Wales |
| 1948 | Ireland |
| 1949 | Ireland |
| 1950 | Wales |
| 1951 | Ireland |
| 1952 | Wales |
| 1953 | England |
| 1954 | England, France & Wales |
| 1955 | France & Wales |
| 1956 | Wales |
| 1957 | England |
| 1958 | England |
| 1959 | France |
| 1960 | England &  France |

| Date | Country |
|------|---------|
| 1961 | France |
| 1962 | France |
| 1963 | England |
| 1964 | Scotland & Wales |
| 1965 | Wales |
| 1966 | Wales |
| 1967 | France |
| 1968 | France |
| 1969 | Wales |
| 1970 | France & Wales |
| 1971 | Wales |
| 1972 | Not Completed |
| 1973 | England, France, Ireland, Scotland & Wales |
| 1974 | Ireland |
| 1975 | Wales |
| 1976 | Wales |
| 1977 | France |
| 1978 | Wales |
| 1979 | Wales |
| 1980 | England |
| 1981 | France |
| 1982 | Ireland |
| 1983 | France & Ireland |
| 1984 | Scotland |
| 1985 | Ireland |
| 1986 | France & Scotland |
| 1987 | France |
| 1988 | France & Wales |
| 1989 | France |

| Date | Country |
|------|---------|
| 1990 | Scotland |
| 1991 | England |
| 1992 | England |
| 1993 | France |
| 1994 | Wales |
| 1995 | England |
| 1996 | England |
| 1997 | France |
| 1998 | France |
| 1999 | Scotland |
| 2000 | England |
| 2001 | England |
| 2002 | France |
| 2003 | England |
| 2004 | France |
| 2005 | Wales |
| 2006 | France |
| 2007 | France |
| 2008 | Wales |

## ALSO AVAILABLE

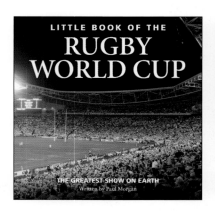

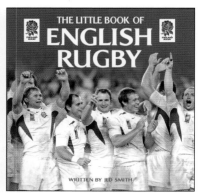

**The pictures in this book were provided courtesy of the following:**

GETTY IMAGES
101 Bayham Street, London NW1 0AG

PA PHOTOS
16 Castle Boulevard, Nottingham NG7 1FL


Design and artwork by David Wildish

Creative Director Kevin Gardner

Published by Green Umbrella Publishing

Publishers Jules Gammond and Vanessa Gardner

Written by Graeme Kent